Poppy Plesiosaur

Look at our readers, Bella! They're soft squidgy creatures from the distant future.

WHOAA! They're really weird looking. And how do they feed themselves properly with so few tentacles?

Bella Belemnite

Alfie Ammonite

To Max, my other consultant palaeontologist – J.E.

To Mum and Dad – A.S.

To my beautiful daughters
Emma and Olivia – A.L.

What are all those strange squiggly symbols?

THE PLESIOSAUR'S NECK is a uclanpublishing book

First published in Great Britain in 2021 by uclanpublishing
University of Central Lancashire, Preston, PR1 2HE, UK

Designed by Becky Chilcott

978-1-9129-7942-4

1 3 5 7 9 10 8 6 4 2

A CIP catalogue record for this book is available from the British Library

Printed and bound in Great Britain by Page Bros Ltd, Mile Cross Lane, Norwich NR6 6SA

How am I supposed to know? I'm an ammonite. I have a brain the size of a pea.

This book belongs to:

. . . .

INTRODUCING:

THE PLESIOSAUR'S NECK

By Dr Adam S. Smith & Jonathan Emmett

Illustrated by Adam Larkum

uclanpublishing

In the age of the dinosaur, deep in the ocean,
the plesiosaur swam with a smooth flapping motion.

Poppy was an *Albertonectes* plesiosaur from the Cretaceous Period, about 73 million years ago. Plesiosaurs were not dinosaurs – they were prehistoric reptiles that lived in the ocean at the same time as dinosaurs lived on land. Poppy was about 12 metres long, about the same length as a bus.

She had much in common with other sea creatures.
She had many regular sea creature features:

four wing-like flippers, broad, flat and strong,
to push through the water and speed her along,

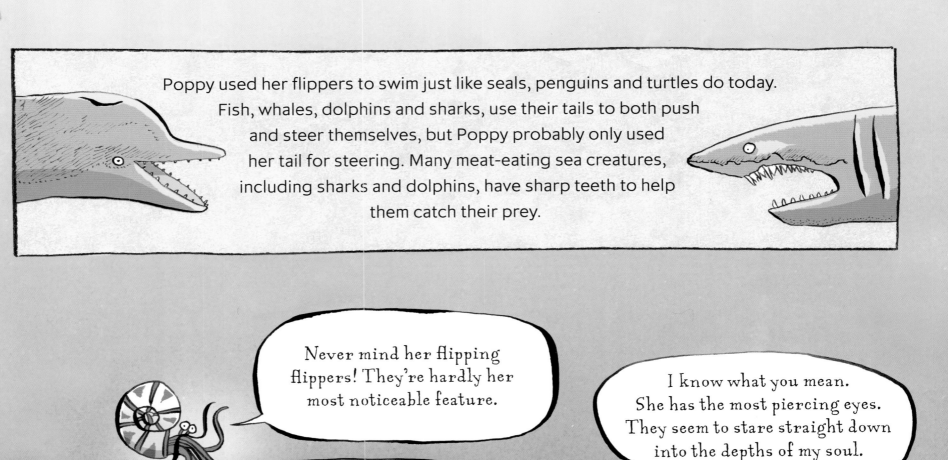

Poppy used her flippers to swim just like seals, penguins and turtles do today. Fish, whales, dolphins and sharks, use their tails to both push and steer themselves, but Poppy probably only used her tail for steering. Many meat-eating sea creatures, including sharks and dolphins, have sharp teeth to help them catch their prey.

Never mind her flipping flippers! They're hardly her most noticeable feature.

I know what you mean. She has the most piercing eyes. They seem to stare straight down into the depths of my soul.

a rudder-like tail, to help steer her way,

and a mouth with sharp teeth, to catch slippery prey.

Oh yes, her neck. I suppose it is a teeny bit on the long side. I spotted that too!

Other types of plesiosaur had long necks but Poppy's type holds the record for the longest!

A fossil of an *Albertonectes* plesiosaur, found in Alberta in Canada, has a seven metre long neck made up of 76 neck bones, more than any other animal ever. The neck of an *Albertonectes* took up almost two-thirds of its entire body length!

THAT RIDICULOUS NECK!

What on Earth was it for?

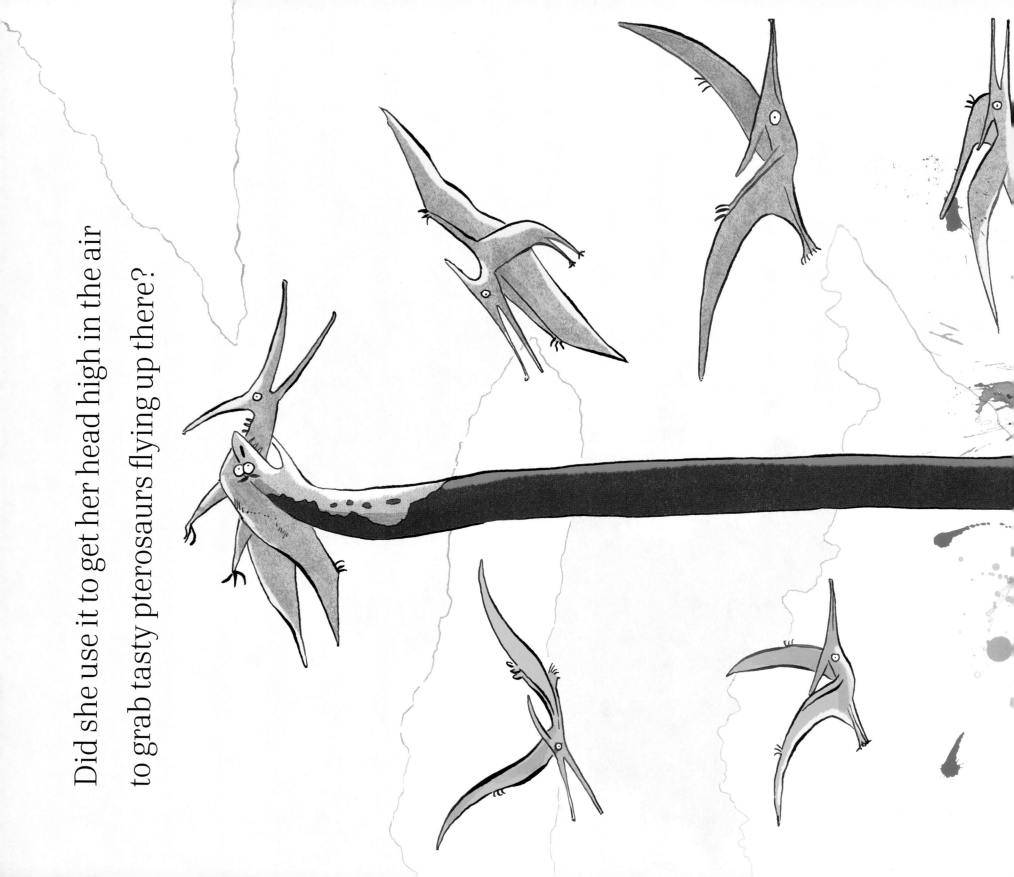

Did she use it to get her head high in the air
to grab tasty pterosaurs flying up there?

Or maybe she used it to reach her backside to pick off small parasites hitching a ride!

Ugh! I would hate to have parasites stuck to my bum!

Yes, they would totally suck!

Many sea animals have to put up with smaller creatures sticking to their skin and even sucking their blood. A long neck might have allowed Poppy to get rid of unwanted passengers like these. However scientists who have studied Poppy's bones think her neck was not flexible enough to reach back to her own body, so she probably wasn't able to pluck prehistoric vampires off her bottom!

It's hard to sneak up with a body that size,

but by swinging her neck, she might spring a surprise.

You might think it would be easy for fish to see a creature Poppy's size coming towards them, but with a seven metre long neck, Poppy could get her small head within biting distance before being spotted. By swinging her neck, Poppy would also be able to move her head around much faster than the rest of her body, making it easier for her to strike at speed and ambush unsuspecting prey.

Coral reefs and seaweed forests are full of tight spots for crabs and other small sea creatures to hide in. Poppy's small head and long neck might have allowed her to reach the places that other large sea creatures could not.

Could she have used it to poke into cracks and delve into tunnels for crunchy-shelled snacks?

Or perhaps it was patterned
to make her look great.

I'm not impressed –
stripes are SO
last season!

An eye-catching neck could attract her a mate!

Scientists are currently unable to tell the exact colour of a plesiosaur's skin from looking at a fossil. If Poppy's neck was patterned or brightly coloured, then having an especially long neck might have helped her to attract the attention of a potential mate, in the same way that a peacock's colourful tail helps to attract a female.

Yes, they haven't been in fashion since the Jurassic Period.

Did she use her long throat to store food in a queue
while she squeezed out the salt, like some sea turtles do?

It sounds *turtley* believable to me!

Although the leatherback turtle, a modern sea reptile, has a very short neck, the food pipe that goes from its mouth to its stomach takes a long winding route and is lined with hundreds of spines. The turtle feeds on jellyfish which contain lots of salty water that would be difficult to digest. As the jellyfish move along the pipe, the unwanted salt water is squeezed out by the spines and spat out of the turtle's mouth. It's possible that Poppy's long neck could have prepared food for digestion in a similar way.

A long neck like that
might have helped her stay lazing,
slumped in a heap while her
head went off grazing.

She looks very comfy, snuggled up in the sand like that.

Yes. I guess that's why they call it the *sea bed!*

It would have taken a lot of food to keep a huge body like Poppy's moving through the water. By leaving her body in one place and just moving her head and neck around, Poppy could save a lot of energy and survive on less food. Some plesiosaur fossils have been found with mussel shells in the stomach, so we know they sometimes fed on slow-moving shellfish that lived on the sea bed.

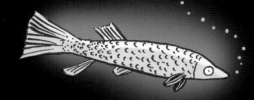

Or perhaps, if a predator saw her as prey,
she could use it to zap them and then swim away!

I can't believe that either! It's a shocking idea!

Plesiosaur necks contained muscles that might have generated electricity like an electric eel, so Poppy's long neck might have been used to stun predators and prey.

I thought it was a stunning suggestion!

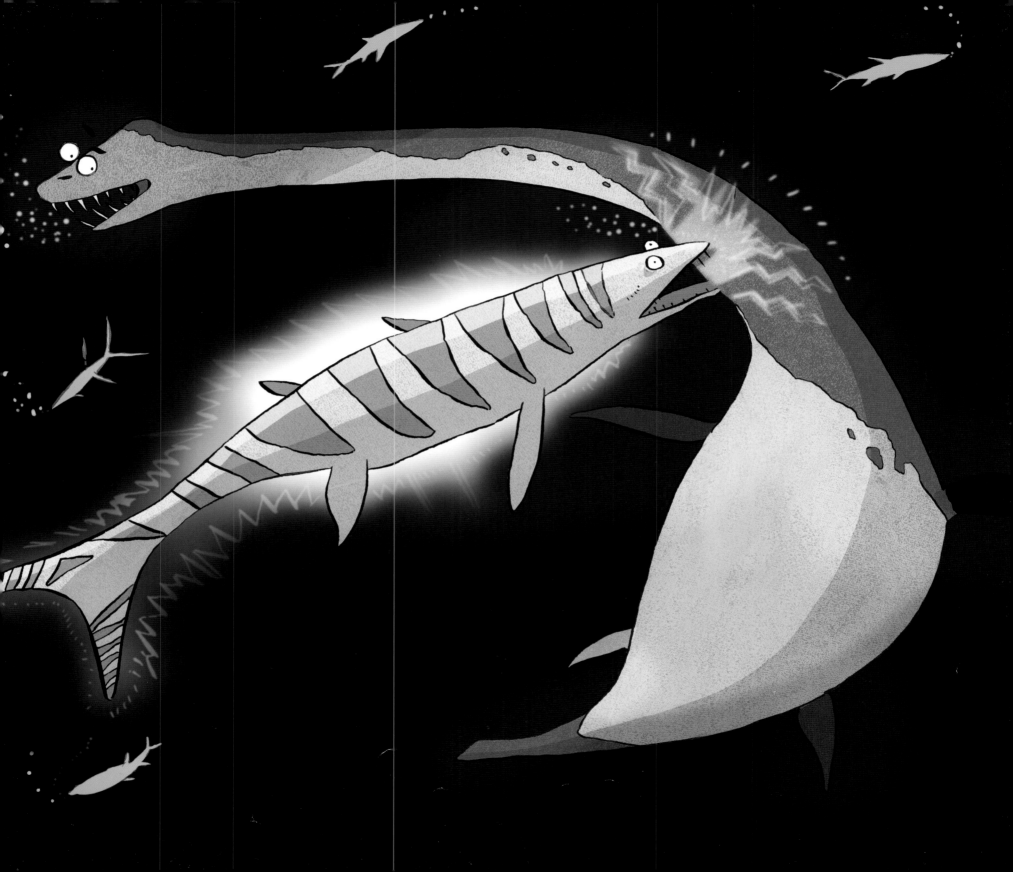

So, what is the answer? We might never know.

We're still searching for clues - it was so long ago.

There are lots of suggestions, but nobody's sure.

So, what do YOU think that immense neck was for?

It is still a mystery why plesiosaurs like Poppy had such extraordinary long necks. The fossils that have been found do not provide enough evidence for scientists to know the answer. Scientists have suggested most of the answers shown in this book. Which suggestion do you think is right? Or do you have an idea of your own?

I can't help noticing that you hogged most of the punchlines in this book.

GLOSSARY

I'm sorry. That was a bit *shellfish* of me.

Albertonectes: An extremely long-necked plesiosaur from the Cretaceous Period. It takes its name from Alberta in Canada where the first fossil of an *Albertonectes* was found.

Ammonite: A prehistoric sea creature related to modern octopuses and squid. The ammonites' spiral shells contained gas to stop them from sinking as they squirted themselves along.

Belemnite: Another prehistoric relative of modern octopuses and squid. Belemnites had long, bullet-shaped bodies and ten hook-covered tentacles to help them grab prey.

Cretaceous Period: The time between 145 million and 66 million years ago.

Electric eel: An eel-like fish that can generate an electric shock to defend itself from predators and stun prey. Electric eels are found in rivers and other freshwater areas of South America.

Leatherback turtle: A large turtle with a thick leathery shell that lives in tropical seas all over the world.

Mate: A partner of the opposite sex that an animal can have babies with.

Parasite: A creature that lives in or on another animal and feeds on it.

Plesiosaur: A prehistoric sea reptile that lived in oceans all over the world. Plesiosaurs first appeared around 203 million years ago and eventually disappeared around 66 million years ago.

Predator: An animal that kills and eats other animals.

Prey: An animal that is killed and eaten by another animal.

Pterosaur: A prehistoric flying reptile with wings made of thin skin. Pterosaurs existed between 228 million years and 66 million years ago.

A SPOTTER'S GUIDE TO THE CRETACEOUS PERIOD

How many of these Cretaceous creatures can you spot inside this book?

Bonefish
(*Paralbula*)

Moss animal
(*Tetrocycloecia*)

Crab
(*Zygastrocarcinus*)

Gar fish
(*Atractosteus*)

Horned dinosaur
(*Styracosaurus*)

Jellyfish
(*Cnidarian*)

Lamprey

Mosasaur
(*Tylosaurus*)

Pterosaur
(*Pteranodon*)

Pug fish
(*Gillicus*)

Sabre-toothed herring
(*Enchodus*)

Sand shark
(*Odontaspis*)

Short-necked plesiosaur
(*Dolichorhynchops*)

Sea turtle
(*Nichollsemys*)

Tyrannosaur dinosaur
(*Daspletosaurus*)

ABOUT THE AUTHORS AND ILLUSTRATOR

DR ADAM S. SMITH is a palaeontologist specialising in the anatomy and evolution of plesiosaurs and has named several newly-discovered species. He is also the Curator of Natural Sciences at the Nottingham Natural History Museum at Wollaton Hall. Adam's neck is 14 cm long and he uses it to turn his head towards interesting fossils. You can find out more about Adam and plesiosaurs at Adam's website **plesiosauria.com**.

JONATHAN EMMETT has written over 60 books for children including *Bringing Down the Moon*, *Someone Bigger*, *The Princess and the Pig* and *How the Borks Became*. His work has been translated into over 30 different languages and has won several awards. Jonathan's neck is 16 cm long and he uses it to transfer coffee from his mouth to his stomach. You can find out more about Jonathan and his books at his website **jonathanemmett.com**.

Over the years **ADAM LARKUM** has built up a variety of clients, working in publishing, editorial, advertising, as well as designing characters for television and working on iPad and iPhone book apps. To date he has fully Illustrated over 50 books and has had a regular column in the *Telegraph* newspaper. Adam's neck is 16cm long and he uses it to rap wooly scarves around it in winter. You can find out more about Adam and his illustration work at **adamlarkum.com**.